To

Dad

HAPPY BIRTHDAY!

love from

Catherine

Xx

DeTour de Yorkshire

Rick Robson

DeTour de Yorkshire

First published in the UK in 2014 by 53x12 Publishing,

Embsay - North Yorkshire

www.53x12.uk

Printed and Bound in North Wales by Cambrian Printers

ISBN 978-0-9930911-0-0

Contents

Rob Partridge - Hartwith

Pete Williams - Park Rash

Introduction

2014 was a once in a lifetime year for Yorkshire cycling with the biggest annual sporting event in the world taking place on our roads, the year following two successive British Tour de France winners.

This book documents some of the routes ridden by Yorkshire based professional riders (past and present) who train amongst Yorkshire's beautiful landscapes through all seasons. Some rides were prior to July 2014 and some were completed after. Each ride includes a section of the TdF stage routes, plus some even more scenic and even harder roads that the TdF could not use... The aim of this book is to inspire with beautiful scenery, rather than a traditional route/map book (although basic maps are included for each ride). This book also offers a glimpse into the lives of the riders.

The area's scenery helped pull me towards cycling when I was 12 years old and joined Bronte Wheelers Cycling Club. The youngsters in the club were in awe of local pro riders Keith Lambert and Sid Barras. It is a great honour to have Sid to agree to write the foreword for this book. As well as being a life long cyclist, I have worked as a photographer / writer since 2008 when I started as a freelancer for CycleSport Victoria in Australia, following a serious cycling accident involving a BIG truck. Since 2009 I have been supplying UK cycling magazines and various organisations with cycling content and images.

2014 is the 20th anniversary of the passing away of one of the best riders Yorkshire has ever produced - Dave Rayner. The fund, set up in Dave's memory, has connections through the majority of riders in this book - 10% of the profits from this book will go to the Dave Rayner Fund.

Rick Robson

Sid Barras - Fleet Moss

Foreword by Dr Sid Barras

Well there you have it. I've been banging on about Yorkshire and the Dales in particular for a long time and in the first weekend in July 2014 everyone got to see what I have been harping on about all these years! The Tour de France showed the world's best cyclists some of the world's best roads and the best in Yorkshire people.

The cyclists featured in this book are luckier than most, being based in some of the finest countryside in the UK. I've been around long enough to have seen so many riders come and go. It's great that cycling unites us all into a family, galvanised in the suffering and the joy of the sport we love. Unfortunately, I am now like the grandparent of the family! This hit home a couple of weeks ago as I led out young Alfie Moses in the sprint at the Cafe Racer ride - FIFTY YEARS younger than me...

The riders that Rick has got together for this book are all vastly different. Annie Simpson revels in the mud and grime of mountain bike racing and cyclocross, Olympic Champion Steven Burke MBE excels at riding at 66kph in the team pursuit and there's a whole host of talented road riders in between. Very different riders, but all united in their love of cycling in the Yorkshire countryside. I can still remember my first venture into the Yorkshire Dales as a 14 year old lad from Middlesbrough. 100 miles including Buttertubs Pass on a fixed gear will be forever etched in my mind...

As founding member of the Dave Rayner Fund, it's also great that this book supports the fund which helps talented young riders take their first steps down the pathway to becoming a professional cyclist. Many of the riders featured in this book have been assisted by the fund.

So be inspired by Rick's beautiful photographs and get out on your bike in Yorkshire - it's the best place to be a cyclist.

Pete Williams

"I live and train in the Yorkshire Dales National Park. When it's sunny and warm there's no place I would rather ride. When the weather is bad in winter - it's really erm, character building..."

- Skipton -

beacon

B6160 to Burnsall

A month after the Tour De France rolled through Skipton, Pete showed me some of his favourite training roads. With the high pressure system planted firmly over the UK for a few weeks, mid summer in the Yorkshire Dales was looking at its absolute best.

In 2012 Pete won the Yodel Sprints jersey in the Tour of Britain and almost repeated the win in 2013. Following some high quality performances in the last few years, the harsh realities of pro cycling have hit Pete pretty hard this year; a freak high-speed accident in the Tour of the Reservoir in April took away a fair chunk of Pete's season and left him with an injury which took months to heal. "Yeah, could have done without it to be honest! It was a strange one, I was riding in the bunch and my hand just slipped off the bars, not sure if it was a dip or grate in the road." The crash left Pete with a broken cheek bone, severe road rash and a hole in his upper back / shoulder.

"You have to play the hand you are dealt, so I've just got on with it really. It's just frustrating that the injury to my back hasn't settled down. It's been really difficult to manage - keeping the wound clean whilst training everyday was hard. It's not like you can have three months off work and recover!" Whilst 'recovering' from injury, Pete raced in the Grand Prix Sarajevo, the Tour of Serbia before heading over to Ireland.

"I was 8th overall in the An Post Ras riding for the French Bretagne Velotec team. I always go well in Ireland - great racing, there's a really nice feel to it. There are races which I would love to do well in, like the Lincoln GP and Rutland Classic. I've been 'up there' in them, it's just timing, having great form and the race falling right - that's all!"

The route chosen by Pete is one which he uses a fair amount through the season and on steady winter rides. "It starts off pretty enough up through Wharfedale. The route back through Coverdale is always a challenge, I think the scenery helps take your mind off it though!"

The first climb up out of Embsay gives immediate impressive views; the valley below is all tranquil except for the Embsay - Bolton Abbey steam train, building up a head of steam before taking its cargo of day trippers down the five mile line.

Once through Upper-Wharfedale, the first categorised climb of the TdF in Yorkshire came into view - 'Cote De Cray' or Kidstones as it is usually known. It isn't a tough climb; it's an easier alternative route to drop into Wensleydale than Fleet Moss. "Great to have a decent look at the writing on the roads," reckoned Pete, "fair play, some of it was quite imaginative!"

The fast descent off Kidstones dropped us into Richmondshire and Bishopdale. The quiet valley road has a really different feel to Wharfedale; the valley is wider and there is more of a sense of space. Once in West Witton, we headed into Coverdale and the gradual climb until the road tops out between Nidd Head and Tor Mere Top. The descent of Park Rash is tricky and includes just about everything you could possibly want in a descent - fast straight bits, fast swoopy bits and a tight, steep hairpin at the end to catch out the over exuberant. Worth taking it easy on there, given the unfortunate combination of no phone reception and the nearest hospital being a good hour away.

"It's harder doing this the other way around - going up the 'hard' side of Park Rash. I did it the hard way with Wilko (Ian Wilkinson), Sam Boast and a few others a while ago. It's not a route to do with a bunch of good riders, it was really hard going," said Pete, wincing as he recounted the challenging day. Park Rash was the scene of Chris Boardman's 1991 National Hill Climb Championship victory, the year before his Olympic Pursuit gold medal in Barcelona. As well as some tough rides with the Lancashire lads and on his own, Pete meets up with the local training group on a Wednesday for a ride up Wharfedale. "It's more or less a race really! They are such a good set of riders, it makes it really hard going.

Kidstones

Kidstones

It's a solid mid week effort though, which probably does us all good when it comes to the weekend races."

Back to civilisation, we dropped into Kettlewell and picked up the quiet lane down the valley through Coniston and Grass Woods into Grassington. The chocolate-box pretty village of Grassington was one of the first places in the UK to have armed local police. Back in the lead mining times of the 1750s, the sleepy village was a rowdy town - its population boosted by shanty towns housing the mine workers - gambling, heavy drinking and general lawlessness ruled the day. A far cry from today. Grassington's only slight brush with modernity, in recent times, was when it was featured in the reality TV show, 'The Village', where contestants vied to win a cottage in the village.

The return ride through Hebden and Burnsall adds more scenic delights to an already stunning ride. The sound of children playing in the River Wharfe was carried up the valley in the still conditions. The very quiet lanes dropped us into Bolton Abbey. Bolton Abbey is a 30,000 acre Woodland Estate owned by the Duke of Devonshire and more importantly for local cyclists, it features the Cav Pav - the Cavendish Pavillion cafe.

Showing the kind of cast-iron determination that won him the TOB Sprints jersey, Pete continued past the Cav Pav and onto a scenic road which has become a local institution, the Gated Road. The gentle climb past Hesketh Farm leads past the farm's sheep, who stoically keep chewing the grass pausing briefly to check out which local pro rider is passing. "Got to finish with the Gated Road! It's the perfect end to a perfect ride!"

Park Rash

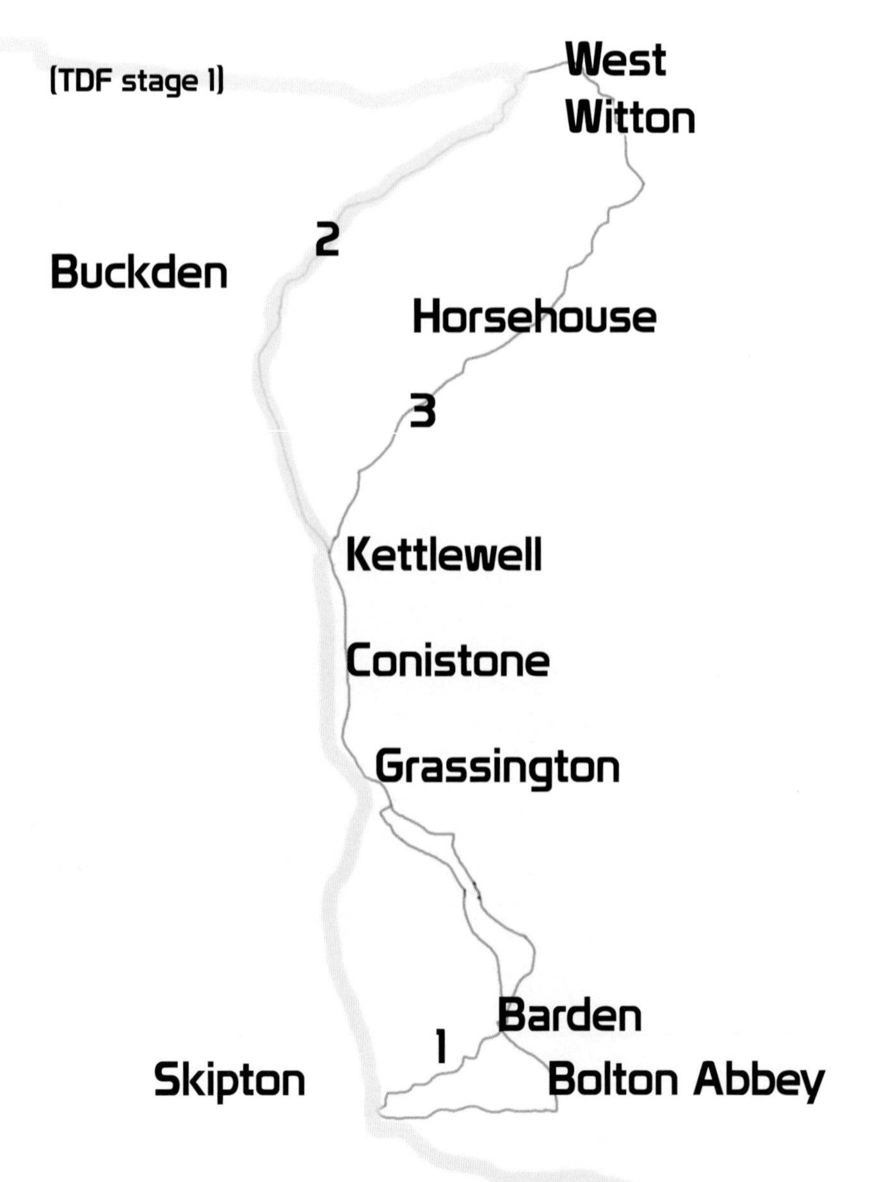

Route Info
72 Miles
10000ft Climbing
TdF Route

Climbs
1 Eastby Crag
2 Kidstones
3 Park Rash

GPX files www.53x12.uk

Skipton - Barden - Grassington - Kettlewell - Buckden - West Witton - Kettlewell - Grassington - Bolton Abbey - Skipton

Burnsall Lane

Joe Moses
Tom Murray

"It's only when I started racing in different parts of the UK that I realised how lucky we are to live and train up here."

Joe Moses

- Kendal -

Joe Moses & Tom Murray - Buttertubs Pass

Dent - Tom Murray (left), Joe Moses (right)

A few weeks before the TdF was due to tackle the Yorkshire Dales, I joined Wheelbase Altura MGD riders, Tom 'Minty' Murray and Joe Moses, on a long steady training ride on their sponsor Wheelbase's Summer Sportive route. The initial roads from Staveley across to Kirkby Lonsdale are constantly up and down – short, sharp efforts designed to warm up the legs before the big climbs kick in. When the route hits Barbon, the long climb breaks out from under tree cover, onto the dramatically scenic Barbon Valley - it is a long slog. Thankfully, the slog is made very rewarding through the truly beautiful Barbondale valley. Once over the top, the steep, tricky descent demanded respect and some decent braking power, before we dropped into the serenity of the Dentdale Valley. "It's only when I started racing in different parts of the UK that I realised how lucky we are to live and train up here," said Joe, as I took his cape which he wore through the low mist on the climb.

Dent is a really quaint, cobbled village with huge character and it was where we had our first break. Both Tom and Joe juggle riding at the highest level and working full time. Tom operates his own cycle coaching and fitness business and also teaches Bikeability within schools. Joe is the middle brother in the Moses cycling dynasty. (Elder brother is Tom - Rapha Condor JLT, younger brother is first year junior Alfie). Joe works full time as a tree surgeon. "Fitting in riding around work can be challenging at times, especially when we're busy, but I really enjoy racing so it's a bit of a balancing act!" said Joe. Tom chipped in, "I am fairly lucky because I can usually juggle work around a bit for training and racing, it usually works out okay."

Out of Dent we followed the River Dee through Cowgill and past the turn off for Coal Road, another well known climb with a reputation for making grown bike riders cry. "Glad we're not going over Coal," I reckon Tom and Joe were thinking...

"It's great scenery up here, really challenging though. I'm riding the 3 Peaks this year so I'll be up here training quite a bit," said Joe. (Joe actually came home 3rd in the 3 Peaks after an eventful race where he survived his bike's fork breaking and had to run to find a spare bike).

Leaving the Dentdale Valley past the viaduct which forms part of the Settle - Carlisle line, we met some German tourists. They were settled in for a long wait to watch a train cross the viaduct. Once we had left them behind and headed up the climb, Tom summoned his best German accent, "the train is due in THREE hours!"

The small town of Hawes was in full Tour De France fever with yellow bikes, cardboard cut-outs of Wiggo and Cav all set for the first weekend in July. Whilst waiting to take a couple of photos on the relatively gentle slopes of Buttertubs Pass, the climb claimed two fallers (yes, going up) from a group of team-building-business types heading over the moorland climb, the day after Chris Froome and some of his Sky team-mates had ridden up. This weekend alone, the climb had seen it all... including three lads on Boris Bikes! When not involved in the biggest sporting event in the world, Buttertubs has extremely light traffic and was once dubbed "England's only truly spectacular road" by Top Gear presenter Jeremy Clarkson.

"Buttertubs is not a hard climb, you do get a few parts where it eases off. It's harder when the weather is bad in winter," reckoned Joe, as we stopped at the top. "The Tour would have been harder over Fleet Moss, but it's a bit tight in places though, I suppose," he added. "Tour of Italy route planners would have done Fleet - they'd have coated it in gravel first though!" reckoned Tom. Once off Buttertubs we turned left, off the TdF stage route, and through Thwaite and Keld before another spectacular stretch of road through Birk Dale and over Nateby Fell. The long steady climb of Nateby Fell finally resulted in a breathtaking vista

Dent Head

Buttertubs Pass

across Cumbria and the Solway Firth – the stretch of water between England and Scotland. The 'Alpine-esque' armco barrier-edged descent is a fast one. Unfortunately, one of the scruffiest sheep in northern England ran out, narrowly missing Joe. He managed a wry smile once disaster was averted! Through the pretty town of Nateby, we headed east through to Soulby and on another stunning stretch of road past the Sunbiggin Tarn, complete with snow marker poles; a reminder to us how exposed and open to the elements this part of Northern England can be.

The village of Orton was in the middle of its annual scarecrow festival which gave us the unnerving feeling of being watched as we headed to the village's tiny chocolate factory. Once Tom had collected his souvenir from the Chocolate factory, we headed north west crossing the M6. South of Shap, we joined the A6 for the ride back to the South Lakes. We had yet more beautiful landscapes to take in - the relentless dragon's teeth profile peaks of the Lake District to the right, the more rolling but equally dramatic Howgill Hills to the left. The homeward stretch towards Staveley had more of the short, sharp climbs which the route started off with nearly 100 miles ago. Back at Staveley, Tom summed up the ride, "Tough ride that one! I think you could only do it with decent weather."

Nateby Fell

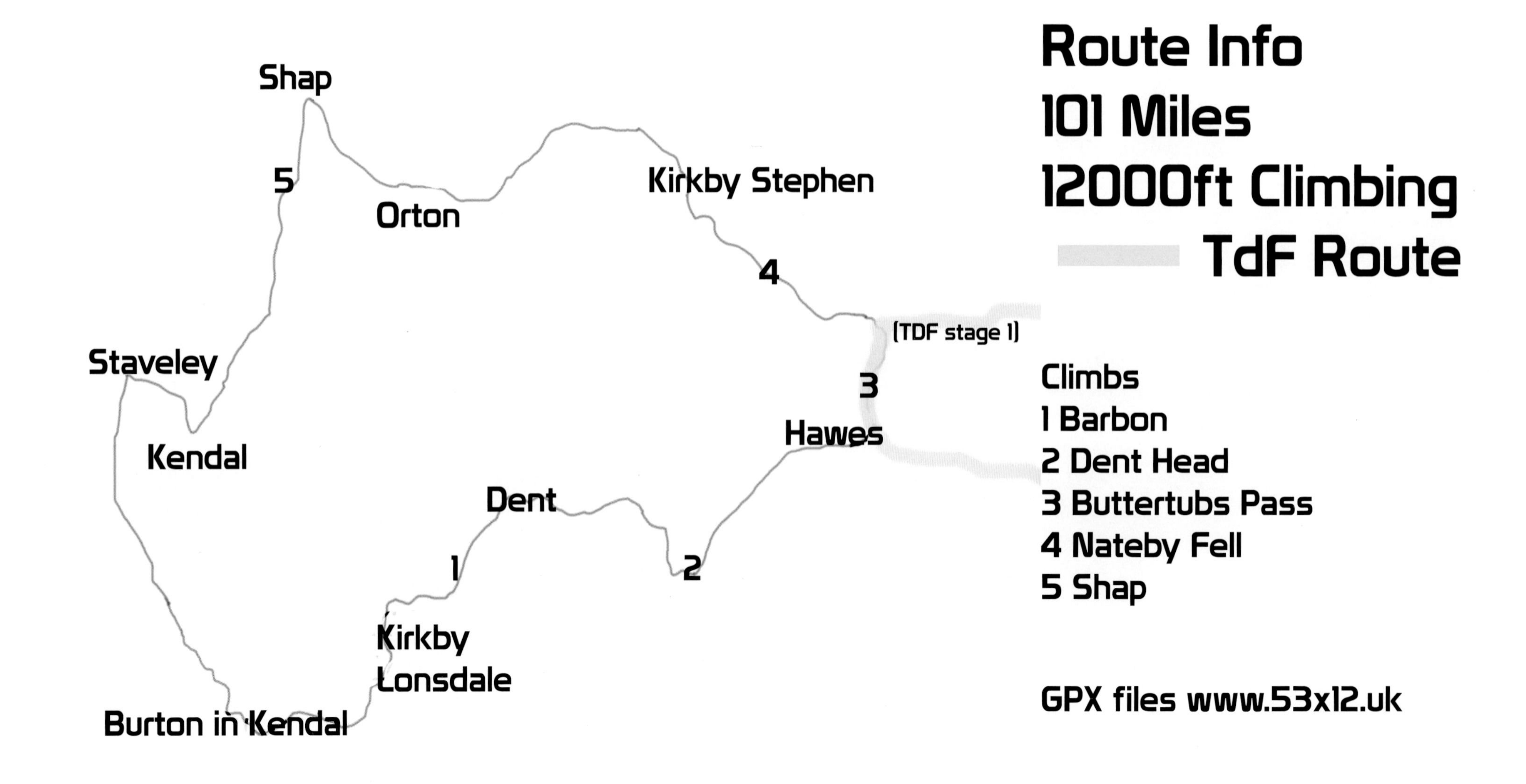

Staveley - Burton - Kirkby Lonsdale - Barbon - Dent - Hawes - Thwaite - Kirkby Stephen - Orton - Shap - Staveley

Buttertubs Pass

Steven Burke

"I go better on the track when I am doing solid road miles too, so rides like this are vital. I get into the Dales a lot - this is one of my regular rides."

- Colne -

Steven Burke - Skipton Old Road

sky
sky
sky
adidas
BRITISH CYCLING
adidas

Olympic Champion in the Team Pursuit, Steven Burke MBE is a real home town hero in Colne, a small, former mill-town which sits just over the county border in Lancashire. His hero status confirmed in the bricks, mortar and tarmac of the new, purpose built Criterium Circuit – The Steven Burke Sports Hub. As well grounded as ever, he still rides the Sunday morning club runs with Pendle Forest CC and inspires the young riders of tomorrow through his involvement in Cycle Sport Pendle, the club which was instrumental in getting the Criterium Circuit off the ground.

We met up a few weeks after Steven joined forces with Sir Bradley Wiggins, Andy Tennant and Ed Clancy to take the Silver medal in the Team Pursuit in the Commonwealth Games, Glasgow. Steven showed me his regular training ride through the Yorkshire Dales from his home town.

“I go better on the track when I am doing solid road miles too, so rides like this are vital. I get into the Dales a fair bit; this is one of my regular rides. It’s good with Pete Williams, my Haribo Beacon team mate living in Embsay, there are some really good riders within a relatively small area – we are lucky that we get to ride here most days!”

From Colne we headed up Skipton Old Road which straddles the county border. “It’s great up here, usually pretty quiet too. When it’s still, you can hear the traffic in the valley below,” reckoned Steven. His involvement in cycling started at a young age. “My Grandad, Brian Wesson, used to race time trials for Pendle Forest CC and my Mum (Sharon Wesson) was racing with the likes of Mandy Jones and the Gornalls in the eighties - so I guess I was always going to be a bike rider! I played football before I got into cycling. I think my Mum was pretty chuffed though when I stopped the football and started cycling. I still support Manchester United, even though it’s got harder in the last year or so!”

I met up with Steven the week after news had filtered through the internet of a team partly backed by Bradley Wiggins, with the sole aim of success in Rio 2016.

"I hope the Wiggins plan comes off, we need to concentrate on World Cup events and Rio Team Pursuit 100%. It's so finely honed now, you can't just turn up after riding Grand Tours or road events for a road team. Each rider has their role and it's very finely tuned. It has been great having Brad back with us - it's great for moral. He is needing to build torque and power for the track now he has finished riding the Grand Tours, but he is such a classy rider. Brad being back gives everyone confidence for Rio."

Once Steven picked his way through the Saturday morning Skipton Market shoppers, the Gated Road between Embsay and Bolton Abbey proved once again to be a great leveller in cycling. The closed gate forcing all riders to dismount and open the gate regardless of Olympic Gold medals... "It's really nice and pretty through here and a great change from the track too," commented Steven.

Up through Wharfedale, the descent into Burnsall saw Steven turn a few heads. "Steven - it's your shout!" came the jokey call from a group of Pendle Forest riders outside the cafe! The flatter roads through Linton took us to Cracoe, where he watched the Tour de France Stage 1. "It was a great atmosphere. I absolutely loved it! So many people watching. It was one of those weekends which you will never forget."

The quiet lanes from Hetton to Gargrave have been the location of thousands of club rides and chain gang 'burn ups' over the years. The lumpy lanes giving lots of opportunities to attack before the wide and long 'Gargrave' sign 'sprint finish' straight - just too tempting for club groups. Once seated in Gargrave Cafe, we had a chance to talk about the Team Pursuit over a toasted teacake.

Gated Road

Gated Road

"It's not easy! Ed (Clancy) starts off so quick, we all go into the red. It's about coping with Ed's fast start and then being able to sit at 66/67 kph for the rest of the 4kms. It's such a unique event there isn't much crossover from other aspects of the sport, so a team where that's the sole aim would be step in the right direction - great for the youngsters coming into the team too. It's such tough competition now. The Aussies probably have more riders to potentially slot into the team, but our core of five or six riders probably have more experience. Jack Bobridge is phenomenal though, but thankfully they've only got one Bobridge!"

The flat lanes through Bank Newton alongside the Leeds Liverpool canal led Steven towards the dark clouds which had started to form over East Lancashire. "Reckon I'll get back in the dry!" shouts Steven, before his smooth track legs speed him home just before the rain closed in.

Burnsall

B6160 from Burnsall

Linton

THE DEVONSHIRE ARMS COUNTRY PUB WITH BEDROOMS
DEVONSHIRE ARMS
AS SEEN ON NATIONAL TV
Big Value Breakfast
Teas, Coffees & Soft Drinks
Energy Drinks "Science in Sport"
Smoothies
Energy / Power Snacks
Great Food
Cask Ales, Wines, Spirits, Rooms
THE DEVONSHIRE ARMS
CASK ALES
GOOD FOOD & WINE
SUNDAY LUNCH
BEER GARDEN
EN-SUITE LODGINGS

Cracoe

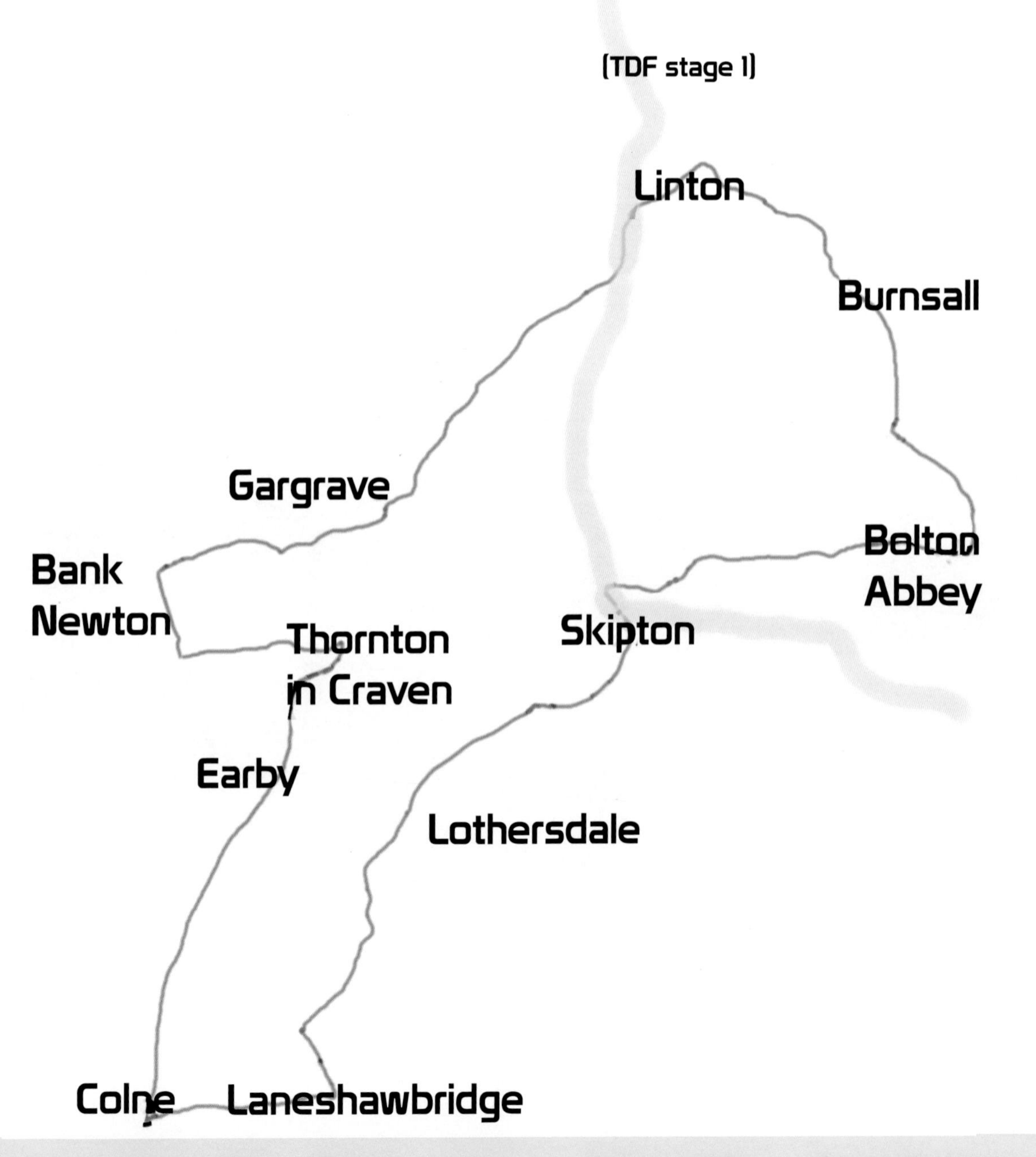

Route Info
48 Miles
5000ft Climbing
TdF Route
(no major climbs)

GPX files www.53x12.uk

Colne - Laneshawbridge - Skipton - Embsay - Bolton Abbey - Burnsall - Linton - Hetton - Gargrave - Bank Newton - Colne

168
Towpath users
Road ahead
Stop
Do not proceed
until it is safe

Bank Newton

Tom Moses

"I am really proud of Keighley and Worth Valley! It's a brilliant place to be a bike rider. Both TDF stages will be hard, the second stage will be something else..."
Tom Moses

- Keighley -

Tom Moses - Cock Hill

The Worth Valley lies in West Yorkshire to the south of the former mill town of Keighley. The most famous village of the Worth Valley is Haworth, which was the home to the Bronte sisters and is a stop on the picturesque Keighley and Worth Valley Railway. Having lived in the Worth Valley until my early twenties, I know the area's roads well.

I met up with Rapha Condor JLT professional rider, Tom Moses, to pedal some of the area's many challenging roads which will soon be sampled by the best bike racers in the world when the Tour de France passes through in July. Following some great results as a Junior, including 6th in the Paris Roubaix, Tom was picked up by the British Cycling for their Academy team 100%ME. Tom then had a year with Raleigh before joining his current team Rapha Condor JLT. "It's a great set up with John Herety in charge - it's easy to have confidence in someone who rode at such a high level as John did. There's a great set of lads in the team too - plenty of banter, but a lot of mutual respect as well."

Having met with Tom in Oakworth, we headed down town to Keighley and out to Steeton by means of a warm up before our hilly tour of the Worth Valley began. The first hill of the day came at the left turn up Barrows Lane, which by rights should be re-named Barras lane. Tom and I wondered how many times Sid Barras, (legendary 70's and 80's rider with 200 pro' wins to his name) would have climbed this hill at the end of a training ride. The mile long climb ramps up sharply in its steeper sections, giving a great view from the top of the Aire Valley north to Skipton and the Dales and south towards Bradford and Leeds.

"Looks stunning today though, they'll be sunbathing in the tarn!" joked Tom as we headed past Redcar Tarn, known locally as Keighley Tarn. The Tarn is also the head of the northern side of the Worth Valley. From the Tarn we dropped into Laycock, before the super steep (over 25%) descent into Goose Eye hamlet. There is a 2 kilometre stretch of relatively flat cobbles heading out of Goose Eye; Tom used the cobbles in training before he rode the Junior Paris Roubaix. "It was pretty ideal, feeling the cobbles fatiguing your body after a tough ride in the Dales!" recalled Tom.

Through Tom's village, Oakworth, we headed down another steep hill, Station Road, which was the setting for a scene of the 1970's TV comedy, Some Mothers Do 'Ave 'Em. Oakworth Station is part of the Keighley and Worth Valley Railway line which was closed by British Rail in 1962. A railway preservation group took control of the line and re-opened it in 1968 and immediately set about styling the station to a 1950's look, which it still has today. The right turn onto Haworth Road put us onto the stage two route of the 2014 Tour de France which passes a stones-throw from the former home of the late Dave Rayner (the former top professional rider, who died tragically in 1994 aged just 27).

Once in Haworth, the short climb of Bridgehouse Lane leads to the foot of Main Street - a short, narrow, cobbled climb which would be an outstanding and atmospheric (but no doubt very crowded) place to watch the race. From Haworth Main Street, a quick tour of the Moors towards Stanbury, and we climbed yet another short, steep hill from Lower Laithe Reservoir over the top of the Bronte Moors. The 'Hollywood Project', provided us with a laugh as we dropped into Oxenhope. Local man, Russell Brown, creates two word phrases in 15 foot high 'HOLLYWOOD' style letters next to a giant bike on the hillside, the current one being, 'DRINK BEER'. Previous ones, 'KNIT WOOL' and 'EAT PIES' have also gone down well.

A sharp right turn in Oxenhope and we were on one of the many longer climbs of the second stage, Hebden Bridge Road, known locally as Cock Hill. The steady, long climb out of the Worth Valley, gave me a chance to ask Tom what he thought, as a UK based professional rider, about the TdF coming to his patch. "It's great, I am really proud of Keighley and

Nab Water Lane

Main Street - Haworth

Worth Valley though! It's a brilliant place to be a bike rider, there are roads we are riding today which I haven't been on for ages, just because there are such a lot of great roads around. Both TdF stages will be hard; the second stage will be something else. There are no classic long climbs, like in the Alps or Pyrenees, but the sheer number of steep climbs, from Keighley onwards, will play a big part in the race."

Over the top of the almost alpine-esque looking Cock Hill, we dropped down towards Hebden Bridge before leaving the TdF route and taking a left at the intriguingly named hamlet of Pecket Well. In Luddenden, we picked up yet another short, steep climb up Stocks Lane, before the long steady climb up Withens Road, passing Warley Wood Reservoir. Dropping back into Oxenhope, we passed Oxenhope Station, the last station on the Keighley Worth Valley railway, and almost the end of the line for our ride as we returned to Oakworth via Providence Lane, yes, yet another short steep climb! The short steep climbs soon add up with over 6000 feet of climbing in less than 40 miles of riding. Little wonder these roads have helped provide the sport of Professional Cycling with some top names in the past, and today - thanks to Tom's exploits. No doubt a whole new generation will be inspired by the sight the World's best riders on their local roads in July.

A few months after this ride, Tom took a brilliantly timed stage win in the Tour of Normandy and won the prestigous Melton - Rutland Cicle Classic. "I think my highlights were Cicle Classic and riding for team mate Hugh Carthy when he won the Tour of Korea. Watching the Tour de France heading through Worth Valley was pretty cool too!" recalled Tom with a smile.

Nab Water Lane

Main Street - Haworth

(TDF stage 2)

Steeton

1

Laycock Keighley

2

Oakworth

Haworth 3

Oxenhope

4

Pecket Well

Hebden Bridge

Route Info
37 Miles
6800ft Climbing
TdF Route

Climbs
1 Barrows Lane
2 Goose Eye
3 Main Street
4 Cock Hill

GPX files www.53x12.uk

Oakworth - Keighley - Steeton - Oakworth - Haworth - Oxenhope - Pecket Well - Oxenhope - Haworth - Oakworth

Condor

Tobyn Horton - Fleet Moss

Tobyn Horton

"I want to come over here on a winter ride. I'll get some of the lads together and have a steady touring-speed ride. Mind you, it never works out that way, someone will start half-wheeling and it would end up carnage - with a 50 mile race home!"

- Grassington -

Kettlewell

Born in Guernsey, Tobyn Horton is a recent migrant to Yorkshire, drawn to the great training roads and quality groups which head out into the Dales. Not the most straight forward route from Guernsey though; Tobyn raced for several years in Belgium, assisted by the Dave Rayner fund, before signing onto various UK teams since. He is currently riding for Madison Genesis.

"Need to get a decent ride in before the Tour of Britain," reckoned Tobyn. I suggested we meet in Grassington and head a bit further into the wilds than his regular training rides. (As it turned out, Tobyn didn't make the team for ToB because of a lingering cold).

From Grassington the route is gentle enough. The valley road through Upper Wharfedale is a gentile affair with relaxing roads. Oughterbridge is where the day's challenges began. The 'easier' side of Fleet Moss is still a tough climb - a selection of steep ramps broken up by easier sections which make it difficult to climb at a steady rhythm. The views from the top are impressive, the immediate foreground is one of the fastest descents in Yorkshire - Fleet Moss towards the village of Gayle. I told Tobyn it was a fast one; I cringed slightly when I snapped him sprinting out of the saddle down the top section - the sound of tyres contacting tarmac at 60mph - easily audible until he was a good mile or so down the descent.

Through Gayle to Hawes, the break from epic northern climbs lasted about twenty minutes until Coal Road. The steep first corner away from Garsdale Station gave way to a slightly less steep climb up past the forest, before more steep ramps delivered the best view across the Dales. We paused on the descent to check out a relic from the Cold War. The nuclear bunker was continually staffed by the MOD until the early nineties before it being decommissioned and sold off. Descending past Dent Station (the highest mainline station in the UK) another flat valley road awaited before the cobbles of Dent. Over a coffee in Dent, Tobyn told me about his recently diagnosed condition. "Yeah, I was diagnosed with Coeliac disease this year. It's a stomach condition which is aggrevated by the eating of wheat / gluten. I actually felt worse when I initially stopped eating gluten! I had to reduce the amount gradually and take a small amount to keep it in balance. There's nothing worse than being ill and not knowing what it is. Once diagnosed, it was a relief really and great to pick up some decent wins this year. Now I have a handle on the condition, it should be easier to manage next year."

Tobyn first represented Guernsey in the 2006 Commonwealth Games in Melbourne where he 'got around' with some decent company including Cavendish, Gerrans and Tuft. "I think I was about 60th. It was great to be racing at that level as a 19 year old." The Commonwealth Games Road Race in Glasgow was a chillier and much wetter race. "Glasgow Commonwealth Games was just a hard wearing-down process, a bit like a really long, wet Crit! Amazing atmosphere though, the crowd was unbelievable when you consider the rain. I was in the top twenty, riding with some decent World Tour team riders, one of them dropped the wheel in front and I had to chase to get back on. It happened a second or third time and that was it - game over. You wouldn't expect those guys to drop the wheel, but I guess it shows how tough everyone found it."

I asked Tobyn which races he enjoyed the most in 2014. "Commonwealth Games were definitely one of the highlights of this year. I had a great week in June too, I won the Canary Wharf Tour Series Crit and the London Nocturne. My condition had settled down a bit and coincided with some good form."

Coffees drunk, we headed out into the early September sun. Not far out of Dent was the start of the most challenging climb of the day - Kingsdale. As well as being steeper and generally poorer quality roads,

Yokenthwaite

Fleet Moss

Kingsdale has the added challenge of gates. Albeit the gates are on flatter parts of the climb, it's still a challenge going from climbing to opening gates and getting clipped in and climbing again.

Luckily, we picked a very rare day in the north Dales, very still and perfect 20 degrees. The Dales were silent and at their stunning best. The Kingsdale view is my favourite in the Dales, it's just a huge amount of moorland but the subtle shades of fields, walls and farms and drop of the climb make it pretty special. A lesser known bit of history which is kept fairly quiet in the local area, offers a spotlight onto a grim period of the past. The dry stone walls searing sharply up from the valley bottom were purportedly built by African slaves kept shackled in the cellar at Whernside Manor, by the Sill brothers (West Indian sugar plantation owners) in the 1700's. Seems bad enough thinking about those forced to build the walls on a perfect summers day - another level of awfulness when you think of the harsh winter conditions which always hit the valley in winter. Documents surrounding Dentdale's hidden history were destroyed when slavery was abolished in the early 1800's. Despite its unpaletable history, the stunning Dentdale and Deepdale landscapes offer some amazing roads to ride.

"I want to come over here on a winter ride. I'll get some of the lads together and have a steady touring-speed ride over here. Mind you it never works out that way, someone will start half wheeling and it would end up carnage - with a 50 mile race home!" The road at the top of Kingsdale is pretty unusual - a pan flat plateaux with a stream - surprising given the height and scale of the surrounding hillsides. By the time Tobyn had dropped into Ingleton, not surprisingly, he had had enough of climbing and so returned on the relatively flat lanes through Clapham, Wigglesworth, Hellifield and Airton. Back in Grassington, Tobyn was feeling the climbs, "Yes, that was a hard ride! Really beautiful though, but we got lucky with the weather!"

Coal Road (Top)

Gayle

Gayle

Coal Road

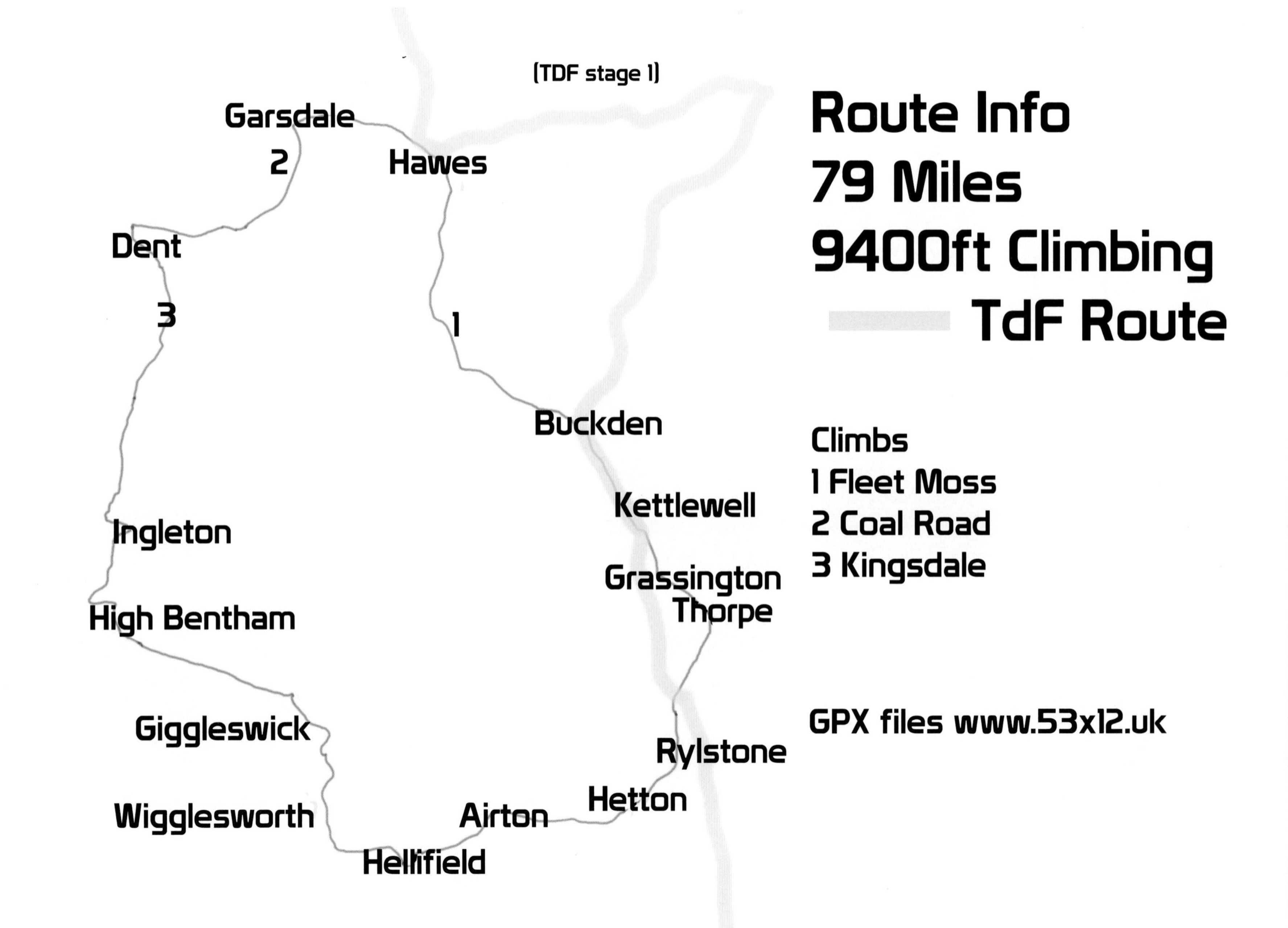

Grassington - Buckden - Hawes - Garsdale - Dent - Ingleton - Giggleswick - Hellifield - Airton - Thorpe - Grassington

Kingsdale

Annie Simpson

"I still get a thrill from climbing the big climbs and reading all the painting on the road. It's very motivational, particularly if your name happens to be 'Froome.'"

- Hebden Bridge -

Annie Simpson - Hebden Bridge Road

hope
hope

The week after the Tour of Britain, I met up with Annie Simpson. She had been working on the Tour Of Britain with her employers OTE. So how was it being on the supporting end of the race? "Oh my god, it was seriously really, really hard! Up at 6.30am everyday, late nights working non-stop, I've ridden tours before and I've got a new respect for the back room staff! It was relentless!"

We met in Hebden Bridge, a pretty and unique town mid way between Leeds and Manchester. The town thrived in the Industrial Revolution; being surrounded by steep hills and fast flowing streams meant the town could benefit from the major wool markets nearby. The town became so well known for garment manufacturing that it was known as Trouser Town.

Annie had a stellar 2012, winning the Tour Series overall and Sprints Classification as well as the National U23 Cross Country in Mountain Biking. Following the completion of her Masters in Sports and Exercise Nutrition, Annie has settled into work as a nutritionist. "It's a balance between work and racing now. It was simpler when I was a student and the spare time after studies was training and racing – I seemed to have more time!"

Each September, just as road riders are looking forward to a few weeks off, Annie's thoughts turn to the mud and filth and the northern cross season together with boyfriend Ian Field, National Cyclocross Champion. "Yeah, it's Ian's fault that I got into cross! I do really enjoy it though. I will be focusing on the National Trophy series this year."

The first climb up Rawtenstall Bank was a tough one, it seems to just keep ramping up higher and higher; the two hairpin corners near the top are the icing on the cake. "What are you doing to me?" joked Annie as she kicked out of one of the cobble-lined hairpins.

The tiny village of Jack Bridge led to another short climb before the left turn to Widdops at Slack Bottom, a village which caused much amusement to Annie's team mate Paul Oldham and me when we came this way for a magazine piece two years ago. Whichever direction Widdops is ridden from, it's a tough ride - challenging roads on their own, but linking them into a loop requires adding lots more climbing and tough moorland roads. "Brilliant training roads over here - it's constantly up and down," commented Annie, mid way up the short steep climb next to Blakedean Scout Hostel.

A herd of massive Highland Cattle added more interest to the slightly murky, grey-day - the big friendly beasts slowly making their way up the valley road towards the reservoir. The silent moorland tops had a real feeling of isolation. Spare a thought for the reservoir-building navvies up there in all seasons through the early 1870's, building the infrastructure to provide the town of Halifax with fresh water eight miles away. The builders relied on gravity to control the flow rather than new fangled pumps.

The descent off Widdops leads into Lancashire. The hills keep on coming before Trawden and Laneshawbridge delivers us back across the border into Yorkshire. The long climb over 'The Herders', named after the pub at the top, brought with it more massive moorland vistas and Watersheddles Reservoir.

Through the village of Stanbury, signs of the summer's brush with a world wide audience at the Tour De France were still visible - yellow bikes and bunting still lingering and a great reminder of those two days in July. "It is just as well the weather was good though!" half joked Annie, given that the week before the Tour came to Yorkshire the weather was definitely not like summer at all. "We watched the first day at Ilkley Cycles on the main street and the second day on the hill out of Keighley. The whole weekend was a bit like a dream. As well as

Widdop Road

Widdop Road

Yorkshire producing some superb weather, there was a real party atmosphere everywhere. It made me so proud to be from Yorkshire and so glad everyone got to see the beauty of it that I have been going on about for years!"

Over Penistone Hill, the Hollywood Art installation stands out as another reminder from the Tour. The installation whilst on Annie's ride was a poignant reminder of the anniversary of the start of the First World War - '1914'. The fifteen foot high white numbers easy to spot on the hillside near Oxenhope.

The next climb over Oxenhope Moor, 'Cock Hill' to locals, was another packed climb in the first weekend in July - the road writing still clearly visible. "I still get a thrill riding up the big climbs and reading all the painting on the road. It is very motivational, particularly if your name happens to be 'Froome'."

Once the climb topped out, so did the weather, as we finally disappeared into to the low cloud which seemed to have been on every hill top of the whole ride. The cloud cleared through Pecket Well and revealed Hebden Bridge, nestling underneath. Annie summarised the ride perfectly, "It is a tough ride, but it's one of those where the views help you forget the pain in your legs. At least the highland cattle were friendly enough!"

Oxenhope

Widdop Road

Lower Laithe Reservoir

Moorside Lane

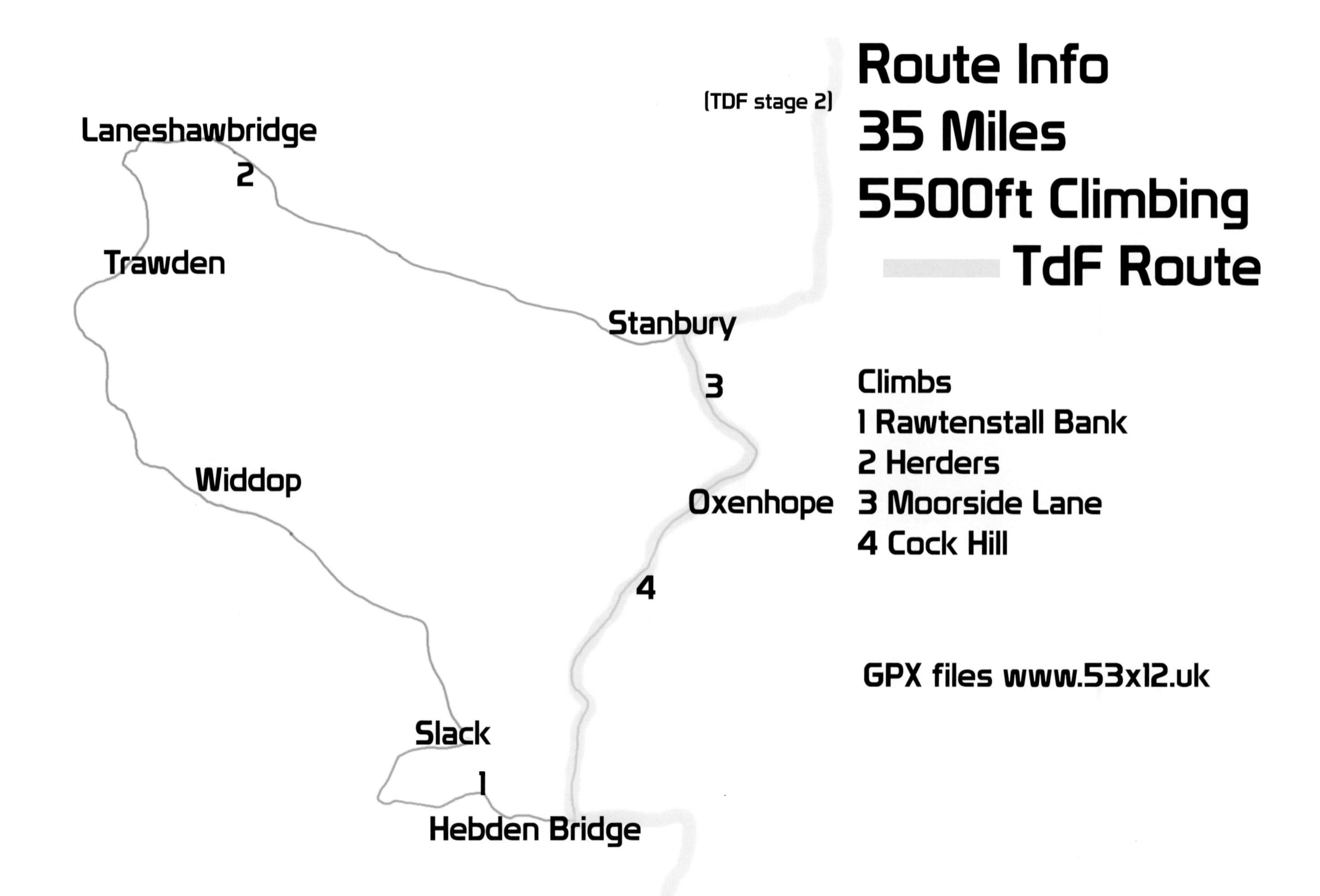

Hebden Bridge - Slack - Widdop - Trawden - Laneshawbridge - Stanbury - Oxenhope - Hebden Bridge

Hebden Bridge

Sid Barras
Tom Barras

"I grew up watching my dad through the barriers at crits and road races – it's all I ever wanted to do."

Tom Barras

- Kilnsey -

Sid (left), Tom Barras (right) - Fleet Moss

Kilnsey

Father and son on the same team is a pretty rare thing. Well, we couldn't think of any others as we headed out for a loop of the roads the Barras duo have virtually made their own over the last forty years. Sid is the experienced Director Sportif behind the Wheelbase MGD Altura team, which his son, Tom rides for.

Sid's experience comes from his 200 professional career wins and 19 years as a pro through the 70s and 80s. A long career only fellow Yorkshire-man Malcolm Elliott has matched. "I should have made a comeback like Malc!" Sid only half jokes. Tom has also had a longer than average UK pro career. "I raced in Belgium full time for six years and then I've ridden for 9 UCI trade teams winning over 100 elite races." When asked about the Barras longevity, the answer is pretty straight forward according to Tom."We both just still enjoy it! If you look after yourself and do the right things, age isn't so much of a barrier. It's great now passing on the things I have learned through my coaching business." (www.training-pro.co.uk)

Even today as a recent new pensioner, Sid is still a very hard rider to drop, according to the elite Ilkley training group which includes current top young guns Scott Thwaites, Tom Murray, Pete Williams, Tom Moses, Josh and Nathan Edmondson and Tom Bustard. "I am a bit biased, but it would be hard to find a more talented training group than what we have on the Ilkley rides," reckoned Tom. "It's a great group - take this weekend for example; there are no races on, so I'll send out a text to the lads for tomorrow and we will have a really hard 'through and off' for a couple of hours which is basically a race in itself. It's great, I reckon even if we didn't race as Pro's, we would still meet up and smash the hell out of each other!" Sid's long, distinguished career as a Pro rider led to him receiving an honorary doctorate from Leeds University. "I'm absolutely over the moon about it. When I got a letter about this, I had to read it half a dozen times before I believed it. You don't expect this sort of thing."

Heading up through Wharfedale and over Kidstones Pass, on the roads which will feature on the first stage of the Tour de France, I asked Sid and Tom what they thought of 'their' roads featuring in the Tour. "It's huge. Brilliant for cycling in Yorkshire, but to be honest, dad was riding these roads forty years ago and we will both be riding them when the Tour's visit to the Dales is a distant memory. It's good that cycling's popularity is so big, but there is a lot of bandwagon-jumping going on too. Let's just hope we get some roads resurfaced!" said Tom. Sid chipped in, "I never wanted to ride the tour. I was happy to be UK based and be successful in a thriving scene, although I picked up stage wins in the Tour of Switzerland and Tour of Mallorca. The UK scene had so much going on back then, with less cars on the roads, single day races like London – Holyhead were great - 275 miles!" Sid continued, "I loved racing in the UK, although my wife, Linda, always said I would end up with a bad back from driving home from races with a wedge of bank notes stuffed in my back pocket! It was a great time in the 70s and 80s. Organisers used to compete against each other to offer the highest prize money, so I never felt like I was missing out by not riding the Tour de France."

The roads of Wharfedale and Littondale have featured heavily in Sid's training since the 1970s. "I used to ride the valleys a lot when I needed speed for crits or flatter road events. I would turn around at the foot of Fleet Moss or Halton Gill and do a lot of fast intense efforts."

Tom was diagnosed with Iliac Artery Endofibrosis in 2011. One leg was only getting 40% of its required blood flow. Four months after corrective surgery, Tom was winning on the bike and feeling good, winning the season-long Yorkshire Road Series in 2012, with solid performances as his body adapted to normality. "I remember back in the 2006 Tour of Britain, a couple of days I was out of the back straight after the Neutralised zone. It's much better now though, I wish I had known about it when I was younger." Health issues aside, Tom has still

B6160 - Kidstones

WHEELBASE
WHEELBASE
cannondale
cannondale

picked up 27 wins since 2007. "I was a stagiere with Linda McCartney team in 2000. When that folded there wasn't much else going on at that time in the UK, so I headed to Belgium at a similar time to Dean and Russell Downing. I ended up staying there for six years." Tom continued, "I grew up watching my dad through the barriers at crits and road races – it's all I ever wanted to do, now the leg's better I hope I can race a few more years and get some decent results."

In between managing various teams since his retirement, Sid has been a cornerstone of the Dave Rayner Fund since the Fund was established. The Fund has helped a long list of riders including David Millar and more recently Dan Martin. "It is really good that something as positive as the fund exists to help young up and coming riders take their riding to the next level". Tom and Sid rode through Thoralby and Bainbridge as we headed to the Wensleydale Cheese Factory Café in Hawes, giving us an opportunity for a coffee and also giving the low cloud over Fleet Moss a chance to clear. "I remember walking up Fleet Moss with Keith Lambert. We had been out on a winter training ride and the snow was getting deeper and deeper – it was un-rideable, we were really lucky to get home that day!"

Once out of the café and onto the slopes of Fleet Moss, I couldn't resist taking a photo of Tom and Sid, recreating those epic scenes from the 1987 Tour of Britain, 170 mile stage to Manchester. Five thousand screaming fans lined the top of Fleet Moss, cheering Sid riding alone as he battled to chase down Dutchman Steven Rooks (PDM) - well worth watching on Youtube. (Also 1977 Glenryck Cup where Sid took a notable second place beating Eddy Merckx).

Back to Kilnsey and Sid summed up the ride nicely, "I'll never get bored of that ride, beats working in an office for a living!"

Yockenthwaite

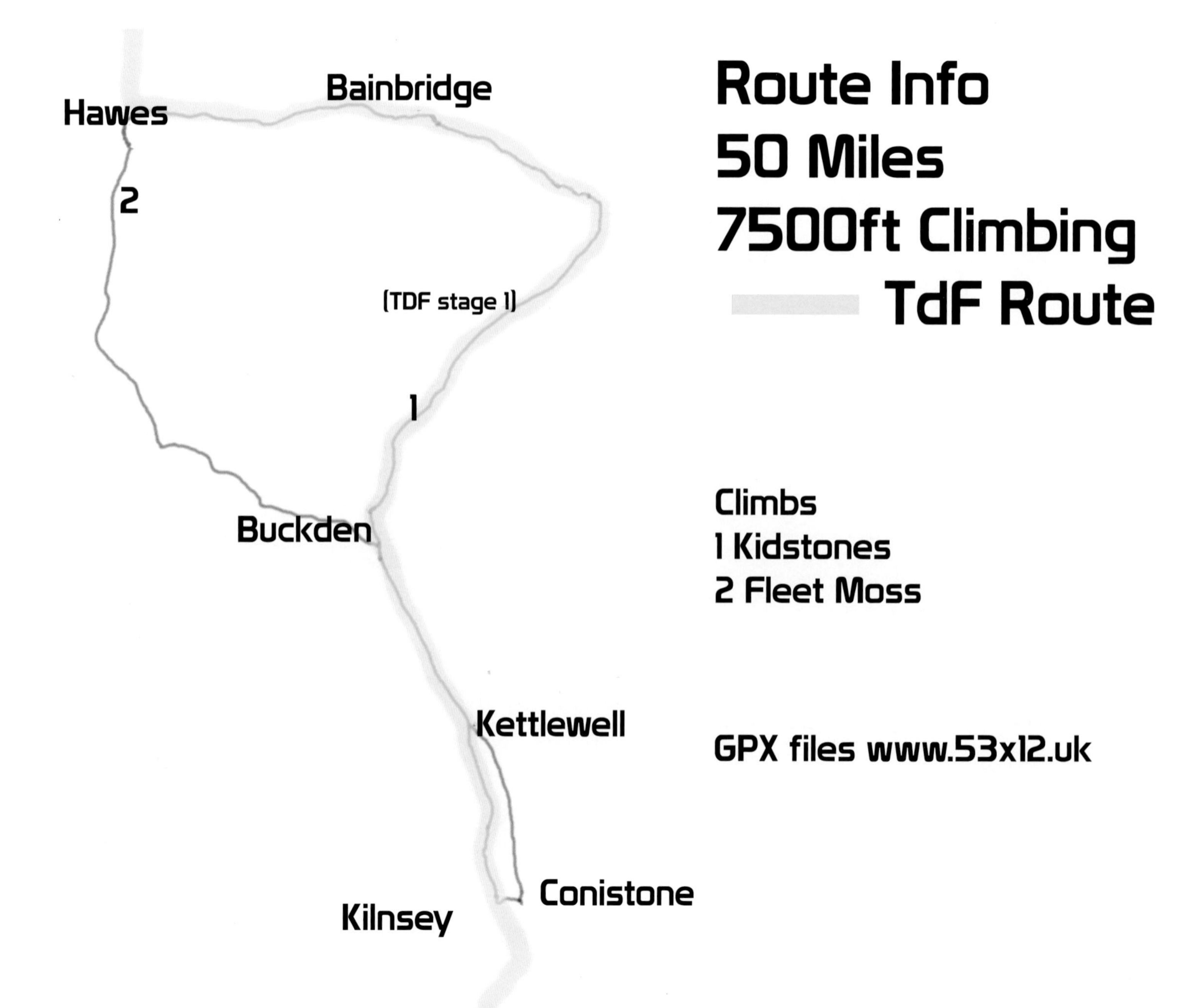

Kilnsey - Kettlewell - Buckden - Bainbridge - Hawes - Hubberholme - Kettlewell - Conistone - Kilnsey

ALTURA
ALTURA
WHEELBASE
WHEELBASE
WHEELBASE
cannondale
cannondale
EVO
SiS
SiS

Fleet Moss

James King

"It was amazing when the Tour came over though. I was in the deep crowds near the cattle grid at the top - amazing weekend, very proud of Yorkshire to be honest."

- Richmond -

James King - Grinton Moor

The Straights - Redmire

“Got his head screwed on right has James,” reckoned Pete Williams, talking about his 19 year old team mate, James King. James is doing a Masters Degree in Geoscience at Durham University. One thing's for sure, he has got some very nice training roads from his parents home in Richmond.

“Yeah, I am pretty lucky really, Richmond is great. We're on the edge of the northern end of the Yorkshire Dales National Park and the flat lands to the east are great for flat, fast riding,” said James before we headed out on one of his regular rides to enjoy some mid August sun.

James was born in Dublin and, as a junior he regularly raced in Ireland. Following some strong results as a junior, he applied for a British passport to allow him to ride the British National Championships. “It made more sense to change to a British passport, rather than having to travel to Ireland for races.”

Riding the big races in 2014 has been an eye opener for James, “It’s been tricky, I always put everything into whatever I do. It’s difficult giving my Masters 100% and racing with top pro riders in the big races. I can win local races but it’s another thing altogether racing against guys whose sole focus is on racing.” James continued, “I'm going to give my studies 100% though. I will be finished when I am 22 – then I will switch to give full time racing a serious go. It's been good to watch Tom Stewart progress, he was in a similar situation with his studies. Realistically that's the best option, to have a decent qualification to fall back on. He’s going to be my test example! He seems to be going really well though and I bet he doesn’t regret getting his qualifications first.”

The quiet tree-lined road from Redmire to Askrigg was the calm before the storm. The right turn before Askrigg led to the first big hill - the long climb over Flow Edge, the same hill range as Buttertubs Pass, but this hill is longer and harder than its neighbour. It’s also got a better view, with Semer Water and the Wensleydale Valley to Hawes in the background.

"It's the longest hill around here, I think. It's also got some real steep sections. Very rare you come across a car up here to be honest!"
The top of the moors gave us some amazing views, shared only with a few very hardcore sheep which must be capable of coping with pretty extreme conditions on the remote hill top.

"This descent is pretty special. It's got it all really, fast bits, tight technical corners, might even get the odd mad sheep - just to keep it interesting!" reckoned James. Regardless of the chance of wayward sheep, it was a photographer's paradise; the heather was at its brightest, dazzling bright purple when the sun popped out.

The valley off to the left is the one the TdF stage one took after Buttertubs Pass. "It's usually a decent tailwind back down the valley, which is nice because I am usually on my way home at that point!"

Rather than join the TdF route in the valley bottom, we turned right for Grinton on the narrow lane which hugged the side of the hill. The hills either side of the route were once again swathed in purple heather. The descent into Grinton was tight and bordering on cyclo-cross with the heavy moorland soil and rainwater washed onto the already tight, tricky, tree covered descent. Clearly not one to take at high speed.

Before heading over Grinton Moor on the TdF route, we popped into the Dales MTB centre for a coffee. I asked James who he looked up to in cycling. "In terms of UK based riders, Scott Thwaites, Pete Kennaugh and the Yates brothers have done some brilliant rides - all really attacking riders who take it to the opposition. I've learned a lot from racing with Pete Williams this year, he has been there and done it, he's a bit like the team Yoda! When we're panicking if things aren't going right, he calms

Flow Edge

High Lane

us down. Steven Burke too, he's such a grounded lad. It's been great for us youngsters and the juniors on the team to have access to riders who have done so much in the sport." I asked James how he thinks he has progressed this year as a rider. "I think I have got mentally tougher and I am getting better at time management. Things like setting goals and targeting specific races are improving. I have learned a lot really; I've learned to enjoy training and recovery which is important, rather than just suffering and turning up to races in a negative mindset. I think I am still developing though. I am getting stronger riding on senior gears, my descending is getting better; I have progressed a lot this year."

After the coffee, it was time to head over Grinton Moor on the TdF Stage 1 route. "I use the other side of the hill more in training, it's more of a steady effort where as this side is a bit on and off. It was amazing when the Tour came over though. I was in the deep crowds near the cattle grid at the top - amazing weekend, very proud of Yorkshire to be honest."

Unfortunately, the fan-art writing on the roads had been tar-chipped the week before we headed over, with just a few bits still visible near the top. It's a shame really – Kidstones and Buttertubs have been left, I think it makes people remember that first weekend in July, although it would be a bit weird scraping snow off 'Go Froome' come the winter snow. The long descent off Grinton soon led to the flatter ride back towards Richmond, the town's castle, dating back to 1071 and the Norman conquest, clearly visible on the horizon. 'James - King of the Castle' - give it a few years and James could well be.

High Lane

HARIBO
beacon

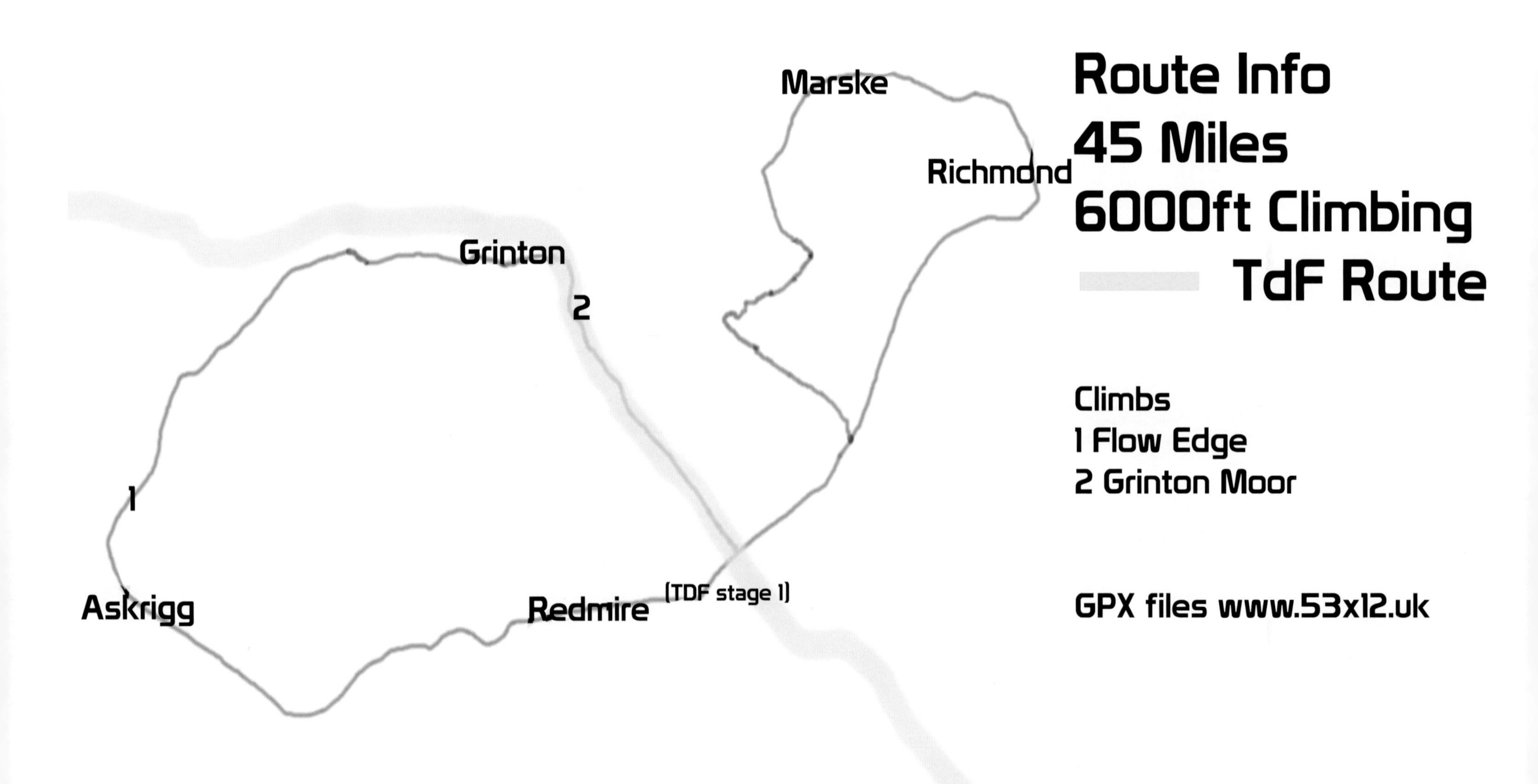

Richmond - Redmire - Askrigg - Grinton - Marske - Richmond

High Lane

Malcolm Elliott - Holme Moss

Malcolm Elliott

"We had raced a lot in Europe through 1987, but I remember the prologue time trial for the Tour was in Berlin, on my birthday. It was horrendously hot and very humid. I was feeling really jaded and I was facing up to three hot and hard weeks of racing the best riders in the world!"

- Sheffield -

As soon as the TdF stage routes were announced, I met up with the legendary Yorkshireman and former Tour de France rider, Malcolm Elliott, to ride a loop incorporating the latter part of the second stage. It was a bit snowy and, to be fair, the five or six miles on the A628 are best avoided. We did the route early on a Sunday morning to minimise traffic.

Malcolm Elliott is Sheffield through and through, proud to hale from the city famous for its steel. However, as we were rolling through the streets where industrial meets residential, with a slightly 'cheaper-end-of-town' vibe on the run-in of the 2014 TdF Stage 2 finish, Malcolm said the words I was thinking. "It's not exactly the Cote d'Azur is it! There are some parts of the route which I would have preferred they would have bypassed, but, that said, it's not easy finding finish locations with parking for 300 trucks and squeezing in Jenkin hill with 2 k's to go. This makes the run-in route more understandable. It's going to be an amazing stage."

Before negotiating the route finish, we headed out on a loop from Malcolm's home in Stannington, from which the 2014 TdF route roads can be seen on the top of the next ridge of hills. "I know, it's a bit unreal that the biggest bike race in the world will be just over there!" With Malcolm's role as Ambassador for the Yorkshire TdF bid team, I was just about to ask if these two facts were related. "Before you ask," joked Malcolm, "I had no input whatsoever on the route passing so near my house! I met the ASO route man a few weeks ago though. I honestly think he's done an incredible job. He's not just drawn on a map, he's writing the script for some amazing drama and, speaking as a local, he's picked some very special roads."

Having first ridden the Tour in 1987, as part of the ANC team, I asked Malcolm what he remembered about the '87 race? "It's unbelievable from where British cycling is now, but I only found out we were riding the Tour two weeks before it started! It was one of the big plans of the ANC team, which we all never really actually thought would materialise. We had

Holme Moss

Giordana
NODE
DMT

Holme Moss

Winscar

raced a lot in Europe through 1987, but I remember the prologue time trial for the Tour was in Berlin, on my birthday. It was horrendously hot and very humid, I was feeling really jaded and I was facing up to three hot and hard weeks of racing the best riders in the world."

From Stannington we headed north, skirting around industrial Stocksbridge and cutting across the edge of Winscar Reservoir to join the stage two route at Holme. "I only came over this way now and again to be honest, more to break up my regular training routes which all headed straight into the Peak District. It's really nice though, quiet and great scenery – I had some decent training options being from the west side of Sheffield."

Heavy snow fall a few days earlier had given a very Alpine look to the ascent of Holme Moss. Once into the snow line, the climb was looking very dramatic with one metre high ploughed snow at the roadside. "It's one of those climbs which will look amazing packed with spectators with 30 k's to go!" I mentioned I had been a spectator in the Leeds Classic on the West Yorkshire climb in the 90s, where I and some mates had created a cheer squad for Djamoladine Abdoujaparov! "He was a one off - Thank god! Yeah, he had a strange interpretation of 'holding your line' in a sprint, I had a few run-ins with him!"

From Holme Moss we joined the main road back to Langsett and the start of a sequence of steep, short climbs. "The Strines from this side is a tricky descent. It's easy to head into the hairpin corner with too much speed." The short and steep Strines climb led to silky smooth section of resurfaced tarmac before we headed off the ridgeline to Oughterbridge and into the teeth of Jawbone Hill. The steep lower slopes are easy to imagine lined with spectators, the gradient eases slightly towards the top. From there the route will take riders down into Sheffield past the giant Meadowhall shopping centre and the final climb of the day over the aforementioned Jenkins Hill. The fact that Tour Director Christian

Prudhomme has described the route as "worthy of Liege-Bastogne-Liege" says it all - it will be a classic stage.

"The sequence of hills in the last hour is going to be perfect. Obviously, most people know how tough Holme Moss is, but to then face The Strines, Jawbone Hill, and then Jenkin Hill just before the finish – it will be very special," surmised Malcolm.

I asked Malcolm if he wishes he was at his peak again to ride the 2014 TdF. "It's funny, it's like when people ask me if I've got any regrets that I wasn't at the peak of my career now. I don't think I would have fitted into the BC and Sky mold to be honest! I did train hard, but I played hard too. I really enjoyed it while it lasted and that's what matters." Malcolm continued, "of course, it would be great if local riders such as Swifty (Ben Swift) or Adam Blythe get to ride. I'm sure it would be very special for them to finish in their home town."

Any regrets at all with his career? "It's a shame my career ended how it did in 1997 (with the Comptel–Colorado Cyclist Team). We had some great youngsters in Levi Leipheimer and Jonathon Vaughters. It was a real shock when the sponsors pulled the pin." He continued, "It's always possible to think I should have won this or that, but I feel satisfied - I had a good career - it was great to come back in 2003 and shake up the domestic scene a bit! It's great to still be so involved with teams and hopefully guiding the up and coming riders through the pro ranks. The UK pro scene is in good shape and it's a pleasure to be part of it."

Penistone Road - High Bradfield

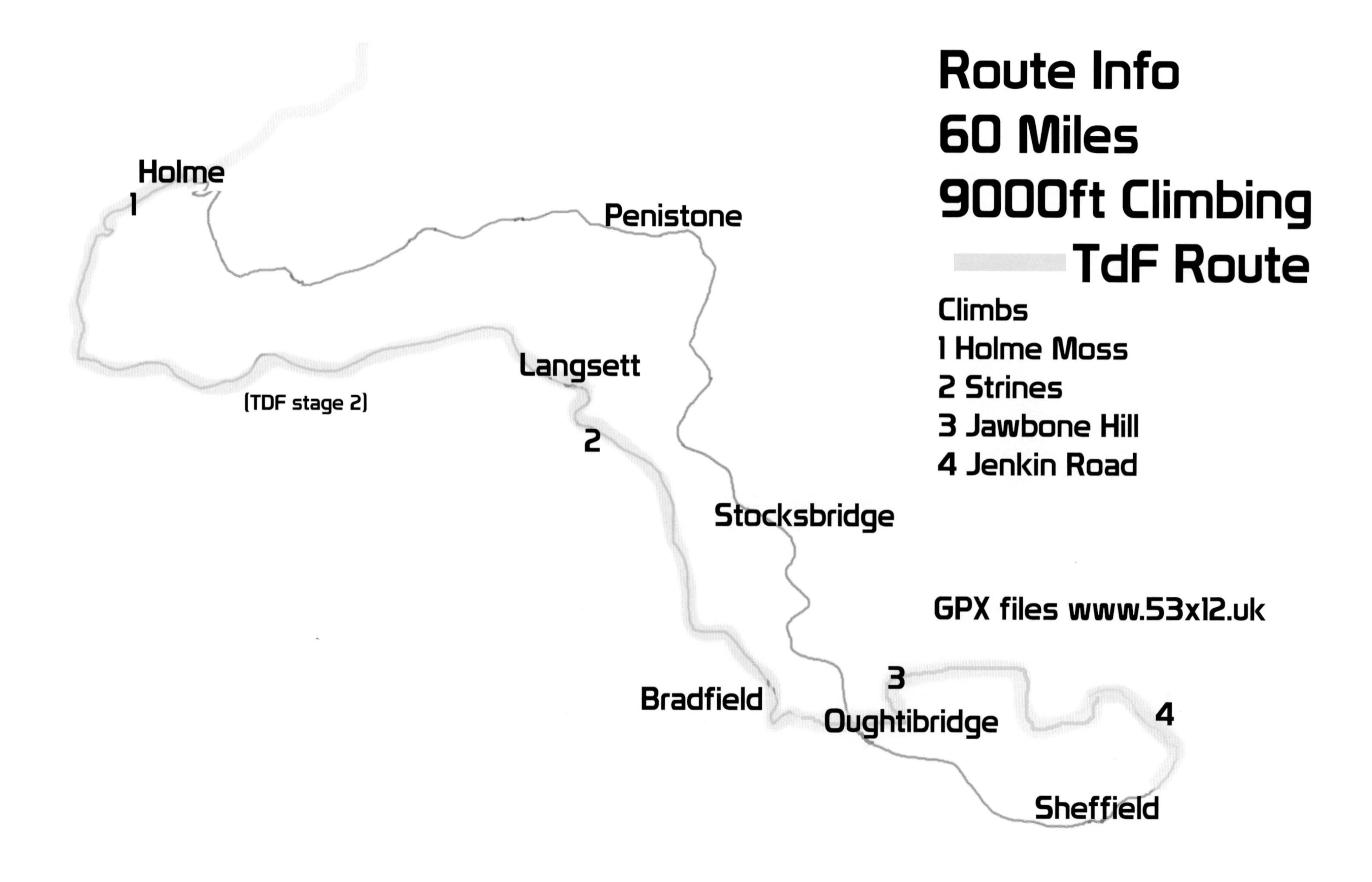

Sheffield - Stocksbridge - Penistone - Holme - Langsett - Bradfield - Oughtibridge - Sheffield

Jenkin Hill - Sheffield

Rob Partridge

"I got in the break on the first road stage of the Tour of Britain. It went through where I grew up. I saw my dad at the side of the road waiting to see me - Oh... Hiya Dad!"

- Harrogate -

Rob Partridge - Peat Lane

Hampthswaite

Having lived in West Yorkshire for the last few years, Rob took me on a tour of some of his favourite training roads before he heads south for the 2015 season.

We started out from the top of Norwood Edge, a well known climb which always features in the northern Hill Climb season. "It's a nice climb Norwood Edge, not massive and not too steep; there's plenty of others in Yorkshire that tick those boxes!" Rob continued, "I grew up in North Wales and there are some hard roads there, it just seems like there are more ups and downs here. Going out training in the Dales, we can struggle to average 30 kph. It does you good though, four hours in the Dales can be like seven hours in other places - I guess it's all quality miles."

Rolling away from Norwood Edge, Rob was soon on the finish drag of the Pennypot Lane circuit. "I've done a few races on here! There was one a couple of years ago and there can't have been much on that weekend. ALL the big hitters turned up and it was ridiculously fast, oh god yeah, bad memories!"

Once through Hampsthwaite, complete with yellow tandems filled with late summer flowers left over from the TdF, the roads once again got hilly through Burnt Yates and the long ascent up Brimham Rocks Road to Hartwith. We passed Brimham Rocks, with its dramatic moorland rock formations, the fast, smooth Ripon to Pateley Bridge road dropped us down into the step-back-in-time town of Pateley Bridge. The quaint little town is home to the oldest sweet shop in the World (Established in 1827). As well as sweets, Pateley also has a little known ultra-steep climb, Peat Lane. The challenging ascent was next on Rob's ride.

"Ha ha, yeah this is insane. I rode this with Wilko (Ian Wilkinson – Raleigh GAC) a while ago. Bad surface, slippery as. It's got to be nearly 30% in the corners - bet it looks a bit epic though!"

Once the ridiculously steep, slippery corners bit was done, Peat Lane stays steep for a while longer, before popping out into more level normality at the Cold Coates sculpture next to the old lead mines high above Pateley Bridge.

A brief stop on the hill top and Rob surveys the valleys below and proclaims, "Really like training up here, that's why I've stuck around really - great lads to ride with. I've been based here for about 5 years or so – it's great for training, harder than most places. It's the constant little hills that make it tough - and big hills too!"

Dropping down towards Stump Cross Caverns, the long stretch of road is a fast one with a few little short ramps to break it up. We took the left turn at Fancarl and passed by Simon's Seat Hill. We negotiated a couple of sharp corners and found ourselves in Wharfedale near Appletreewick. The very quiet lanes on the east side of the River Wharfe led us to the Cavendish Pavillion cafe. I asked Rob how he got into the sport.

"I watched the TdF on telly, that kind of got me interested in cycling. It was the year Pantani won, I think. Turned out my early cycling heroes weren't quite legit! Eventually, my dad got me a bike. All I can remember was it was too big for me and New Year's Day 1999 I was descending a big hill in North Wales and the skin on my fingers had frozen to the metal brake levers! After that I was hooked!" joked Rob.

"I've had a steady progression as a cyclist; I rode the Junior Tour of Wales way back in 2003 and got to ride internationally as a junior and an under 23 rider. It's all about learning the ropes as a young rider and picking up wins. 2010 was a real break-through year, I did some decent rides all year, culminating in taking 8th on General Classification at the Tour of Britain.

B6265 - Ripon - Pateley Bridge Rd

Brimham Rocks Road

Looking back on 2014, I asked Rob what his highlights were.

“Jock Wadley was a really good win. I played it exactly right and had decent form. You have to take your chances when you are going well. The Nationals was another good ride; I was the first UK-based rider in 7th behind the Sky lads and the Yates’. The really tough circuit suited me and it was great to be amongst the big teams. There’s been good moral at Velosure Giordana though and it’s great when a nice set of lads get good results all year.”

So how was the Tour of Britain? “It was great, but really, really tough. I got in the break on the first road stage. It went through where I grew up. I saw my dad at the side of the road waiting to see me - Oh Hiya Dad! It was great with lots of local support out. It was a really extra hard TOB this year - a combination of the route and all the riders having their own reasons to ride hard and try to get in the action. It seems to get more serious and important each year.”

“It was pretty special watching the Tour de France on Buttertubs too, so atmospheric - just amazing. On Stage 2 we were on the big wall near Stanbury which was also great. A genuinely amazing weekend.”

Leaving the Cavendish Pavillion behind, the last few miles included the tough moorland climb of Langbar and the back lanes through Ilkley and Denton to Otley, the quiet flat lane at the side of the River Wharfe providing a rare break from the ‘ups and downs’ of the rest of the ride. The final climb of the day and Rob made short work of Norwood Edge. “Yeah, these are great training roads. When you’re trying hard and suffering, there’s always some nice bits of scenery to cheer you up!”

Peat Lane

Hazler Lane

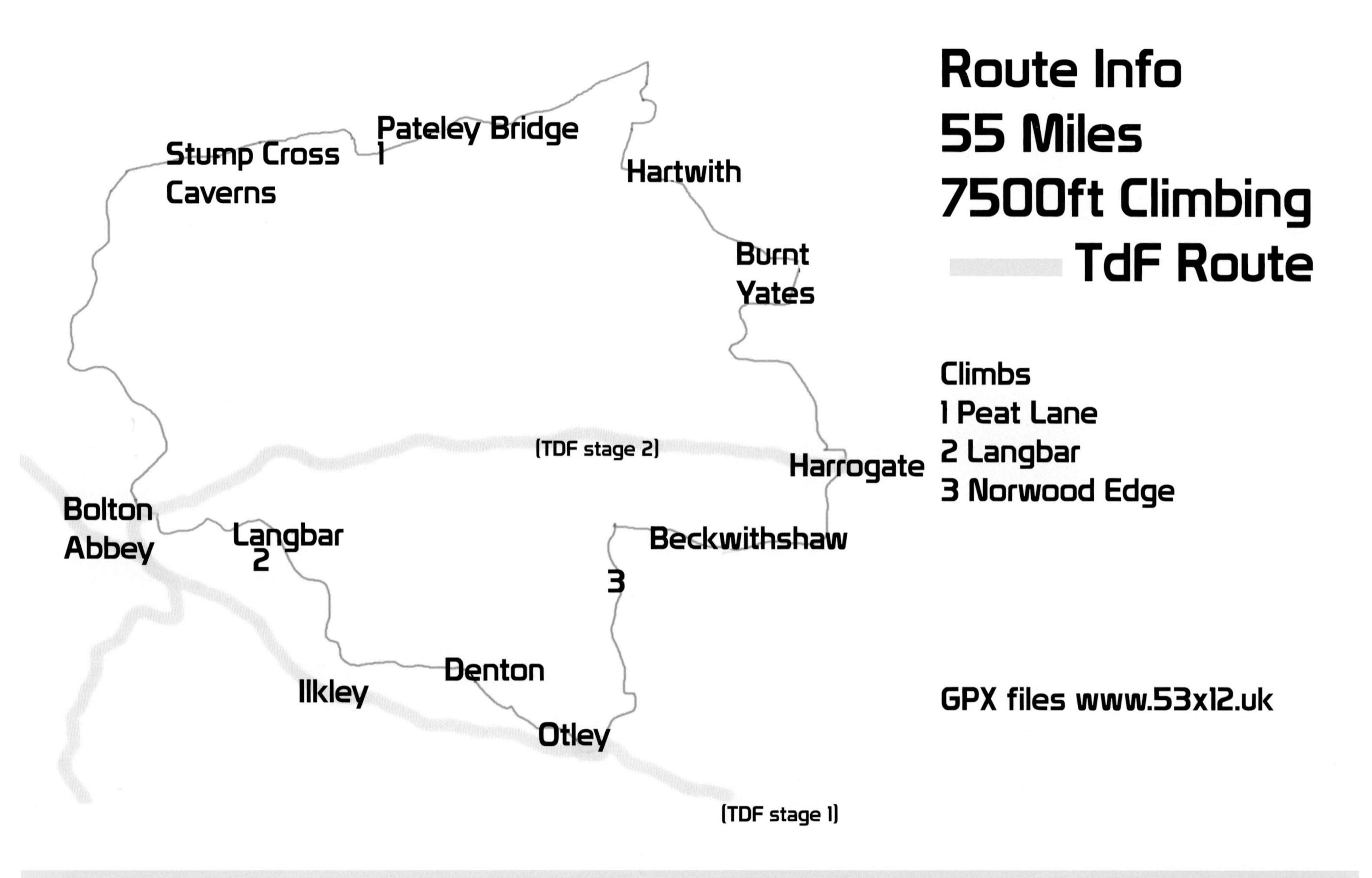

Beckwithshaw - Burnt Yates - Pateley Bridge - Stump Cross - Bolton Abbey - Langbar - Ilkey - Otley - Beckwithshaw

Norwood Edge

Jack Pullar (right) & James Gullen (left) - Jubilee Tower

Jack Pullar & James Gullen

"Yeah, it's not a bad place to ride! Depending what you want from your training, fast and flat / rolling hard / proper hilly – we've got it all to be honest." James Gullen

- Lancaster -

Cragg Wood

Firstly, this ride is, strictly speaking, not in Yorkshire and technically, James and Jack live in Lancaster. However, James is originally from Leeds and half the ride would have been in the West Riding of Yorkshire before the boundaries got fiddled with in the 1970s! Aside from that, Bowland and North Lancs is one of the best places to ride a bike in the UK and favourite UK training roads of Sir Bradley Wiggins.

Jack and James are two Pro riders who, as well as having the ability to win road races and get a pro contract, can also climb hills fast. Jack specialises in short, steep power climbs and James loves the long, steady climbs. Jack won the Hillclimb Champs in 2012 and James was runner up in 2013. "It makes training hard when Jack goes hard on the short climbs, but then I make him suffer too – so it's all fair!" said James.

The rapid duo are based in Lancaster with some impressive training options - South - the flat, fast lanes of central Lancashire, North – the dramatic Lake District, East - the Forest of Bowland / North East Lancs, which was our destination for this ride with plenty of hills to suit both riders.

The Bowland / North East Lancs region was a right of passage for northern club riders through the ages. A destination of choice for a tough day out from West Yorkshire, North Yorkshire, Merseyside, Central and East Lancashire. The Trough of Bowland was often the centrepiece of many a club rider tale of daring-do. Wyresdale Road out of the city centre, in a way, sets the tone for the ride. It's a hill to the side of the very impressive Williamson Park with its impressive Ashton Memorial – a 150 foot high dome folly which overlooks the city, built by industralist, Baron Ashton. Wyresdale Road, in most rides, would be THE hill. In this ride it's not even the nibbles before the starter... "Yeah, it's not a bad place to ride! Depending what you want from your training, fast and flat / rolling hard / proper hilly – we've got it all to be honest. As luck would have it, the spread of climbs suited both Jack and James fairly equally.

The descent after Wyresdale Road leads into the first long proper climb, Jubilee Tower. "I was the first rider to get under seven minutes on Jubilee. It just goes on and on at the top – it's not my ideal climb – too long!" said Jack. He went on to explain his love of the short power-blast climb. "Yeah, I'm a two minute man - short and intense that's me! When I won the National Hill Climb in 2012, I won it on pure speed at the bottom of the Rake (Ramsbottom, Lancashire) and I just hung on up the steep bit. It was my best day and worst day in cycling. Becoming National Champion was great, mega publicity, but I really hurt myself to win it, I've never felt that bad." I was witness to Jack's pain, taking photos for Wheelbase, Jack's sponsor at the time. I felt bad capturing Stu Reid, Wheelbase team captain, holding a bucket for Jack to throw up into and Jack, ashen-faced and ill-looking, being helped to walk to the race headquarters to get on top of the podium. If anyone deserved to win that day, it was Jack.

The view from the top of Jubilee is great and makes the climb well worth it. When it's clear you can see Blackpool and across Morecambe Bay to the Peaks of the Lake District. The descent off Jubilee leads to a beautiful flat section under the trees next to the river. "It's a really pretty little section this. I think it's what most people remember about the Trough of Bowland, aside from the deep V of the trough itself," reckoned James. The rolling lanes through the step-back-in-time villages of Dunsop Bridge and Newton lead to Slaidburn and the turn off for the climb of Cross of Greet. "It's a 'Quiet Lane', except for your legs screaming out in pain when it kicks up!" After a few miles, once you get to the cattle-grid, the climb makes itself apparent, winding its way up and across the fell. "It's one of those climbs that looks harder than it actually is. Goes on a bit though," remarked James, with a glint in his eye.

The descent off Cross of Greet is a fast and fun one, swooping down into a stunning landscape of rolling Lancashire goodness. A quick stop in Wray gave me a chance to ask the lads what their highlights of the 2014 season were. "Commonwealth Games Road Race," was Jack's quick response. (He

Dunsop Bridge, Cross of Greet

Cross of Greet

rode on the Scottish team). “It was like a really hard Kermesse rather than a road race, but it was a really emotional event. People were constantly shouting 'Scotland' at me the whole way around. It was goosebumps all day – amazing. It was a once in a lifetime experience.”

“I went to watch the TdF stage one, over near Ripon,” said James. We were on just a random bit of road on our own, a few hours before the race was due. As the day went on, more and more people came. By the time the race came through it was rammed! Brilliant day, again it was a once in a lifetime experience. Race wise, I've had a few decent wins this year. I think the OOTS Road Race was the best one, decent competition and I played my hand exactly right, away in a group of three, then just kept attacking and attacking until I was on my own – brilliant.”

The lads knew what was coming up. “Not been over there for ages – it’s the roads you battle over in winter,” winced James. I knew the roads from the Le Terrier Sportive which takes place every June, organised by Lancaster CC's Graham Orr, coincidentally the man responsible for getting Jack into cycling.

Roeburndale doesn't see much car traffic. It doesn't see many cyclists either, mainly thanks to the very steep ramps up out of the valley and the rough gravel, and the four closed gates, and the cows! When you put all the challenges of Roeburndale together, it makes for a tough ride. If you are with others, it’s worth gauging your climb to get them to open the gate. “It’s so hard, that's why we don't do it that much. It’s relentless.”

The climb up Scout Camp was the next tough section. I think the lads had had enough climbing at that point as they jokingly started head butting each other up the climb! Another stunning scenic vista though; the dome of the Ashton memorial clearly visible on the horizon. So with one last steep climb for good measure (Stocka Bank), we returned to Lancaster contemplating the best bits of Lancashire and Yorkshire. “It is all good though, isn’t it?” summarised James. Couldn’t have put it better myself.

Roeburndale

STARLEY

Velosure
STANLEY PRIMAL
CORIMA

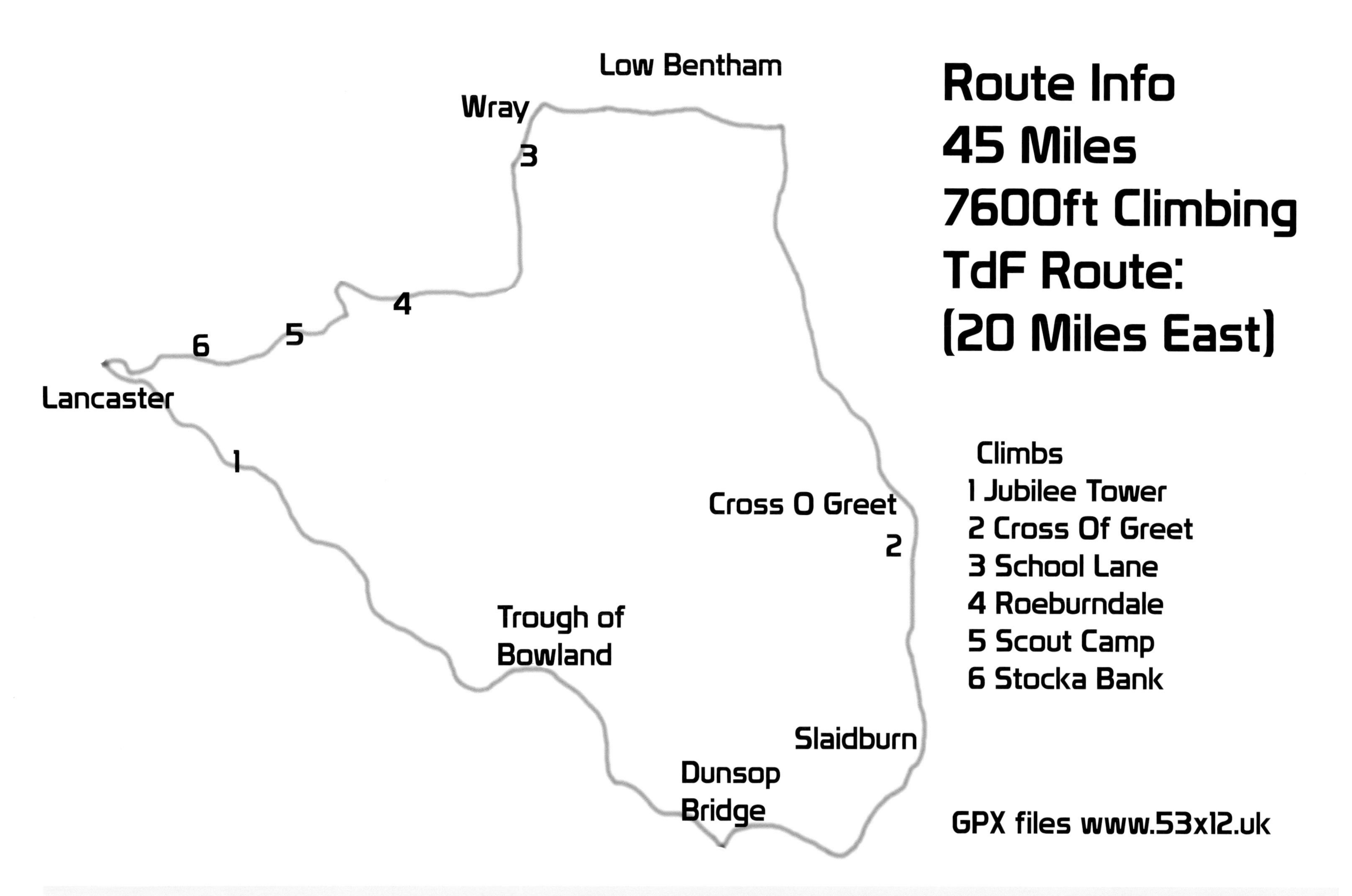

Lancaster - Quernmore - Dunsop Bridge - Slaidburn - Cross Of Greet - Wray - Roeburndale - Crossgill - Lancaster

WHEELBASE
MGD
cannondale
sky

MADISON
GENESIS

Tour de France 2014 Stage 1 Starbotton

Tour de France 2014 Stage 2 Stanbury

Tour de France 2014 Stage 1 Starbotton, Stage 2 Stanbury

Thanks to...

Sid Barras
Tom Barras
Malcolm Elliott
Tom Moses
Steven Burke MBE
Joe Moses
Tom Murray
Pete Williams
Jack Pullar
James Gullen
James King
Tobyn Horton
Annie Simpson
Rob Partridge